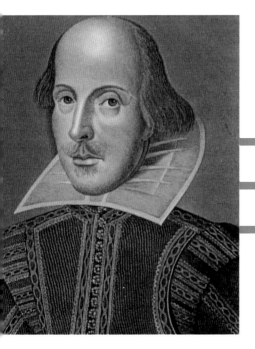

A
MUSE
of FIRE

A SHAKESPEAREAN JOURNAL

WITH ILLUSTRATIONS FROM
The Huntington Library
San Marino, California

POMEGRANATE ARTBOOKS   *San Francisco*

Front cover: *Hamlet's Soliloquy*, Watercolor illustration for *Hamlet*, unattributed.

Published by Pomegranate Artbooks
Box 6099, Rohnert Park, California 94927

© 1994 Pomegranate Artbooks

Illustrations © 1994 The Huntington Library, Art Collections and Botanical Gardens, San Marino, California

ISBN 1-56640-995-0
Catalog No. A762

Pomegranate publishes several other illustrated journals, as well as books, address books, calendars, notecards, posters, bookmarks and postcards. For information on our full range of publications, please write to Pomegranate, Box 6099, Rohnert Park, California 94927.

Designed by Bonnie Smetts Design
Printed in Korea

INTRODUCTION

O for a Muse of fire, that would ascend
the brightest heaven of invention . . .

The opening line from Shakespeare's *Henry V* is as tantalizing and
compelling today as it was when it was first performed, but to the
modern listener it reverberates with a cadence that seems novel to the
ear. Simply put, it is distinctly Shakespearean.

For those of us who have ever marveled at a modern stage or film
interpretation—whether it be Sir Laurence Olivier's Othello or, of more
current acclaim, Kenneth Branagh's Henry V—it is easy to overlook the
fact that we, too, are versed in Shakespeare—only in more subtle ways.
In fact, we can assert our incredulity at such a notion by "knitting our
brows" and, "without rhyme or reason," proclaim "it's Greek to me."
Many are simply left "tongue-tied." Whatever the case may be, these
phrases have reached beyond the exclusive repartee of playwright and
actor to become part of our everyday speech. With Shakespeare, we have
"made a virtue of necessity," and "that is the long and short of it."

It is noteworthy that in an age when Latin was the predominant
language for the dispersal of knowledge throughout continental Europe,
William Shakespeare opted for a renaissance in his own language. After
all, this was an age of reformation and discovery; a time when national
pride was at stake as England vied with the countries of Europe for an

ever-greater portion of an unchartered globe on the one hand, and begrudged the pope's authority over the inhabitants of England on the other. Thus, it was in a spirit of discovery and national pride that Shakespeare became a great innovator of the English language and, in doing so, imbued it with what Samuel Johnson would later call "the diction of common life."

Upon the release of Shakespeare's First Folio in 1623—seven years after his death—new words appeared in print for the first time. At the height of his genius, Shakesepeare commanded a vocabulary in excess of 30,000 words, much of which he fabricated to suit his own purposes. He experimented freely and borrowed from other languages and dialects to create a distinct and enduring lexicon and was attuned to the nuances of language, from contemporary rhetoric to classical. Words such as *dislocate, obscene, premeditated* and *assassination* are but a few of Shakespeare's contributions to our vocabulary.

There is little doubt that Shakespeare's use of language is unparalleled to this day. His plays exhibit the range of his abilities, from the more farcical and bombastic verse found in the early comedies *The Taming of the Shrew* and *The Two Gentlemen of Verona* to the more refined verse of the later comedies *A Midsummer Night's Dream, Much Ado About Nothing, The Merchant of Venice* and *As You Like It*; to the more complex characters and political situations found in the great historical plays *Richard II, Julius Caesar, King John* and Parts 1 and 2 of *Henry IV;* and the great problematic characters and moral dilemmas in the tragedies *Hamlet, Macbeth, King Lear, Othello* and *Antony and Cleopatra*. His mastery of blank verse, poetry and prose, in addition to his extensive vocabulary, combine to make the whole of his work singularly revolutionary.

The illustrations for this journal are drawn from a variety of sources in the rare book collections of the Huntington Library, a scholarly research institution located in San Marino, California. The majority of the illustrations, including all of those identified as original watercolor drawings, are reproduced from *The Turner Shakespeare,* a unique forty-four–volume extra-illustrated edition of Shakespeare's works compiled by Thomas Turner of Gloucester early in the nineteenth century.

The Huntington collections include many illustrated editions of Shakespeare's plays, but the most important of the Huntington's Shakespeare holdings are its superb collection of early quartos and folios of the plays, a collection that is the equal of the three other great collections, those of the British Library, the Bodlein Library and the Folger Shakespeare Library. Eighteen plays appeared in quarto before Shakespeare's death, published in forty-six various editions. Of these very rare books the Huntington has thirty-seven of the forty-six editions and all thirteen of the quarto editions printed after Shakespeare's death and before the publication of the First Folio in 1623. The Huntington has twenty-nine copies of the seventeenth-century folios of the plays. Shakespeare left no extant manuscripts of his work, and there exists much speculation about the accuracy and authority of varying early printed editions. The Huntington collections have been of great importance in efforts to arrive at an authoritative text for the plays.

I would have thee gone:
And yet no farther than a wanton's bird,
Who lets it hop a little from her hand,
Like a poor prisoner in his twisted gyves,
And with a silk thread plucks it back again,
So loving-jealous of his liberty.

—ROMEO AND JULIET, *Act II, Scene ii*

Romeo and Juliet
Watercolor illustration by John Masey Wright (1777–1866) for *Romeo and Juliet*

In nature's infinite book of secrecy
A little I can read.

—ANTONY AND CLEOPATRA, *Act I, Scene*

Our remedies oft in ourselves do lie,
Which we ascribe to heaven.

—ALL'S WELL THAT ENDS WELL, *Act I, Scene i*

But long it could not be
Till that her garments, heavy with their drink,
Pull'd the poor wretch from her melodious lay
To muddy death.

—HAMLET, *Act IV, Scene vii*

The drowning of Ophelia
Illustration by W. G. Simmonds for *Hamlet,* 1910

What stronger breastplate
than a heart untainted!

—HENRY VI, Part 2, *Act III, Scene ii*

Double, double, toil and trouble;
Fire burn and cauldron bubble.

Fillet of a fenny snake,
In a cauldron boil and bake;
Eye of newt and toe of frog,
Wool of bat and tongue of dog,
Adder's fork and blind-worm's sting,
Lizard's leg and howlet's wing,
For a charm of powerful trouble,
Like a hell-broth boil and bubble.

—MACBETH, *Act IV, Scene i*

The witches
Engraving by Henry Fuseli (1741–1825) for *Macbeth*

The lunatic, the lover and the poet
Are of imagination all compact.

—A MIDSUMMER NIGHT'S DREAM, *Act V, Scene*

Teach not thy lips such scorn, for they were made
For kissing, lady, not for such contempt.

— RICHARD III, *Act I, Scene ii*

King Richard III
Pen and watercolor illustration by Robert Dighton (1752?–1814) for *Richard III*

Come what come may,
Time and the hour runs through the roughest day.

—MACBETH, *Act I, Scene iii*

But love is blind, and lovers cannot see
The pretty follies that themselves commit.

—THE MERCHANT OF VENICE, *Act II, Scene vi*

O god of love! I know he doth deserve
As much as may be yielded to a man:
But Nature never framed a woman's heart
Of prouder stuff than that of Beatrice.

— MUCH ADO ABOUT NOTHING, *Act III, Scene i*

Beatrice overhears Hero and Ursula
Watercolor illustration by John Masey Wright (1777–1866) for *Much Ado About Nothing*

How beauteous mankind is! O brave new world,
That has such people in't!

Blow winds, and crack your cheeks! rage! blow!

You cataracts and hurricanes, spout

Till you have drench'd our steeples, drown'd the cocks! . . .

Rumble thy bellyful! Spit, fire! spout, rain!

Nor rain, wind, thunder, fire, are my daughters:

I tax not you, you elements, with unkindness. . . .

Here I stand, your slave,

A poor, infirm, weak, and despised old man.

—KING LEAR, *Act III, Scene ii*

King Lear, the Fool and the Earl of Kent in the storm
Watercolor illustration for *King Lear,* unattributed

I will walk up and down here, and I will sing,

that they shall hear I am not afraid.

— A MIDSUMMER NIGHT'S DREAM, *Act III, Scene i*

Quince startled by the transformation of Bottom
Illustration by Arthur Rackham for *A Midsummer Night's Dream*, 1908

O, what men dare do! what men may do! what
men daily do, not knowing what they do!

—MUCH ADO ABOUT NOTHING, *Act IV, Scene i*

When you shall these unlucky deeds relate,

Speak of me as I am; nothing extenuate,

Nor set down aught in malice: then must you speak

Of one that loved not wisely but too well.

— OTHELLO, *Act V, Scene ii*

The murder of Desdemona
Watercolor illustration by John Masey Wright (1777–1866) for *Othello*

My words fly up, my thoughts remain below:
Words without thoughts never to heaven go.

—HAMLET, *Act III, Scene iii*

Did Cicero say any thing?

Ay, he spoke Greek.

To what effect?

. . . those that understood him smiled at one
another and shook their heads; but for mine own
part, it was Greek to me.

—JULIUS CAESAR, *Act I, Scene ii*

Cicero
Pencil drawing for *Julius Caesar,* unattributed

Let there be gall enough in thy ink, though
thou write with a goose-pen, no matter.

—TWELFTH NIGHT, *Act III, Scene ii*

I know thee not, old man: fall to thy prayers;

How ill white hairs become a fool and jester!

—HENRY IV, Part 2, *Act V, Scene v*

The King berates Falstaff and banishes him from his company
Pen and watercolor illustration by John Augustus Atkinson (1775–active until 1833) for *Henry IV, Part 2*

Safely in harbour

Is the king's ship; in the deep nook, where once

Thou call'dst me up at midnight to fetch dew

From the still-vex'd Bermoothes, there she's hid.

— THE TEMPEST, Act I, Scene ii

Ariel bringing into harbor the King of Naples' ship
Illustration by Arthur Rackham for *The Tempest,* 1926

For to the noble mind
Rich gifts wax poor when givers prove unkind.

—HAMLET, *Act III, Scene i*

Alas, poor Yorick! I knew him, Horatio:

a fellow of infinite jest, of most excellent fancy:

he hath borne me on his back a thousand times;

and now how abhorred in my imagination it is!

— HAMLET, Act V, Scene i

Hamlet with the skull of Yorick
Illustration by W. G. Simmonds for *Hamlet*, 1910

Our doubts are traitors,
And make us lose the good we oft might win
By fearing to attempt.

—MEASURE FOR MEASURE, *Act I, Scene iv*

Then came wandering by
A shadow like an angel, with bright hair
Dabbled in blood; and he squeak'd out aloud,
"Clarence is come; false, fleeting, perjured Clarence
That stabb'd me in the field by Tewksbury:
Seize on him, Furies, take him to your torments!

—RICHARD III, *Act I, Scene iv*

Clarence's dream
Watercolor illustration by John Masey Wright (1777–1866) for *Richard III*

I must have liberty
Withal, as large a charter as the wind,
To blow on whom I please.

—AS YOU LIKE IT, *Act II, Scene vii*

What's this? "To the Pope!"
The letter, as I live, with all the business
I writ to 's holiness. Nay then, farewell!
I have touch'd the highest point of all my greatness;
And, from that full meridian of my glory,
I haste now to my setting: I shall fall
Like a bright exhalation in the evening,
And no man see me more.

— HENRY VIII, *Act III, Scene ii*

Henry confronts Cardinal Wolsey with Wolsey's letter to the Pope
Watercolor illustration by John Augustus Atkinson (1775–active until 1833) for *Henry VIII*

What's in a name? that which we call a rose
By any other name would smell as sweet.

—ROMEO AND JULIET, *Act II, Scene ii*

With love's light wings did I o'er-perch these walls,

For stony limits cannot hold love out:

And what love can do, that dares love attempt;

Therefore thy kinsmen are no let to me.

—ROMEO AND JULIET, *Act II, Scene ii*

Romeo and Juliet
Watercolor illustration attributed to "Johnson" (active 1830) for *Romeo and Juliet*

Till thou canst rail the seal from off my bond,
Thou but offend'st thy lungs to speak so loud;
Repair thy wit, good youth, or it will fall
To cureless ruin. I stand here for law.

—THE MERCHANT OF VENICE, *Act IV, Scene i*

Shylock anticipating his pound of flesh
Engraving by Cook for *The Merchant of Venice* from an original drawing by Ramberg

Though this be madness,
yet there is method in't.

—HAMLET, *Act II, Scene ii*

Where's the king?

Contending with the fretful elements;

Bids the wind blow the earth into the sea,

Or swell the curled waters 'bove the main,

That things might change or cease; tears his white hair,

Which the impetuous blasts, with eyeless rage,

Catch in their fury, and make nothing of;

Strives in his little world of man to out-scorn

The to-and-fro conflicting wind and rain.

KING LEAR, *Act III, Scene i*

Lear in the storm
Watercolor illustration by W. K. Beecham for *King Lear*

Love looks not with the eyes, but with the mind;
And therefore is wing'd Cupid painted blind.

—A MIDSUMMER NIGHT'S DREAM, *Act I, Scene i*

I prithee, do not strive against my vows:
I was compell'd to her; but I love thee
By love's own sweet constraint, and will for ever
Do thee all rights of service.

— ALL'S WELL THAT ENDS WELL, *Act IV, Scene ii*

Bertram importunes Diana
Watercolor illustration by John Masey Wright (1777–1866) for *All's Well That Ends Well*

Love thyself last: cherish those hearts that hate thee;
Corruption wins not more than honesty.

—HENRY VIII, *Act III, Scene ii*

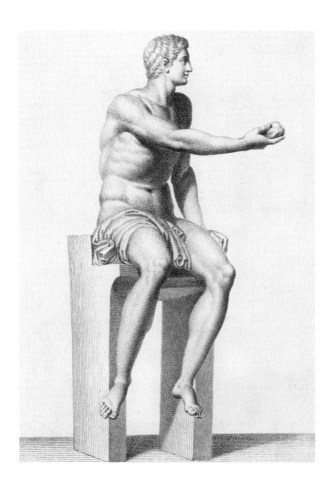

He eats nothing but doves, love, and that
breeds hot blood, and hot blood begets
hot thoughts, and hot thoughts beget hot
deeds, and hot deeds is love.

— TROILUS AND CRESSIDA, *Act III, Scene i*

Paris proffers the "Apple of Discord"
Engraved illustration for *Troilus and Cressida,* unattributed

Weaving spiders, come not here;

Hence you long-legg'd spinners, hence!

Beetles black, approach not near;

Worm nor snail, do no offence.

— A MIDSUMMER NIGHT'S DREAM, *Act II, Scene ii*

The Fairies sing Titania to sleep
Illustration by Arthur Rackham for *A Midsummer Night's Dream*. 1908

Silence is the perfectest herald of joy: I were
but little happy, if I could say how much.

—MUCH ADO ABOUT NOTHING, *Act II, Scene i*

Counterfeit? I lie, I am no counterfeit: to die, is to
be a counterfeit; for he is but the counterfeit of a
man who hath not the life of a man: but to
counterfeit dying, when a man thereby liveth, is to
be no counterfeit, but the true and perfect image of
life indeed. The better part of valor is discretion; in
the which better part I have saved my life.

—HENRY IV, Part 1, *Act V, Scene iv*

After counterfeiting his death, Falstaff rises and looks with fear on the slain Hotspur
fearing that he, too, has feigned his death
Watercolor illustration by John Masey Wright (1777–1866) for *Henry IV, Part 1*

When beggars die, there are no comets seen;
The heavens themselves blaze forth the death of princes.

—JULIUS CAESAR, *Act II, Scene ii*

So sweet a kiss the golden sun gives not
To those fresh morning drops upon the rose,
As thy eye-beams, when their fresh rays have smote
The night of dew that on my cheeks down flows:
Nor shines the silver moon one half so bright
Through the transparent bosom of the deep,
As doth thy face through tears of mine give light;
Thou shinest in every tear that I do weep.

— LOVE'S LABOUR'S LOST, *Act IV, Scene iii*

Biron hides in a tree as the King, Longaville and Dumain read sonnets
Watercolor illustration by John Masey Wright (1777–1866) for *Love's Labour's Lost*

There are more things in heaven and earth, Horatio,
Than are dreamt of in your philosophy.

—HAMLET, *Act I, Scene v*

Ay me, I see the downfall of our house!
The tiger now hath seized the gentle hind;
Insulting tyranny begins to jet
Upon the innocent and aweless throne:
Welcome, destruction, death, and massacre!
I see, as in a map, the end of all.

— RICHARD III, *Act II, Scene iv*

*The Dowager Queen of Edward the 4th
parting with the Duke of York to the two archbishops*
Hand-colored engraving by Francis Bartolozzi for *Richard III*

Wear this for me, one out of suits with fortune,

That could give more, but that her hand lacks means.

— AS YOU LIKE IT, *Act I, Scene ii*

Rosalind giving her chain to Orlando
Watercolor illustration by John Masey Wright (1777–1866) for *As You Like It*

If thou remember'st not the slightest folly
That ever love did make thee run into,
Thou hast not loved.

—AS YOU LIKE IT, *Act II, Scene iv*

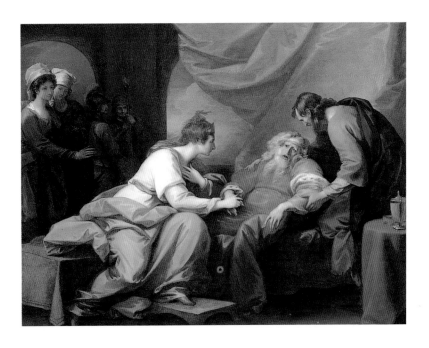

You do me wrong to take me out o' the grave:
Thou art a soul in bliss; but I am bound
Upon a wheel of fire, that mine own tears
Do scald like molten lead.

— KING LEAR, *Act IV, Scene vii*

The Meeting of Lear and Cordelia
Oil on canvas, 42½ x 57 in., c. 1784, by Benjamin West

Brevity is the soul of wit.

—HAMLET, *Act II, Scene ii*

To be, or not to be: that is the question:

Whether 'tis nobler in the mind to suffer

The slings and arrows of outrageous fortune,

Or to take arms against a sea of troubles,

And by opposing end them.

— HAMLET, *Act III, Scene i*

Hamlet's soliloquy
Watercolor illustration for *Hamlet,* unattributed

When Love speaks, the voice of all the gods
Make heaven drowsy with the harmony.

—LOVE'S LABOUR'S LOST, *Act IV, Scene iii*

Give me my robe, put on my crown; I have
Immortal longings in me: now no more
The juice of Egypt's grape shall moist this lip.

— ANTONY AND CLEOPATRA, *Act V, Scene ii*

The death of Cleopatra
Colored engraving after a drawing by Paul Avril for *Antony and Cleopatra,* 1891

One touch of nature makes the whole world kin.

—TROILUS AND CRESSIDA, *Act III, Scene iii*

Yes, I thank God I am as honest as any man living

that is an old man and no honester than I.

— MUCH ADO ABOUT NOTHING, *Act III, Scene v*

Leonato with Dogberry and Verges
Watercolor illustration by J. Coghlan (active early nineteenth century) for *Much Ado About Nothing*